DRUMMER'S SURVIVAL GUIDE

PRE-PREPPED CHARTS FOR WRITING, TEACHING, LEARNING & REFERENCE

COMPILED BY BART ROBLEY

ISBN 978-1-57424-252-2
SAN 683-8022

Book Design by Roy David Dains / London West Advertising
www.londonwestadvertising.com

Copyright © 2010 CENTERSTREAM Publishing, LLC
P.O. Box 17878 - Anaheim Hills, CA 92817

www.centerstream-usa.com

 TABLE OF CONTENTS

NOTATION KEY

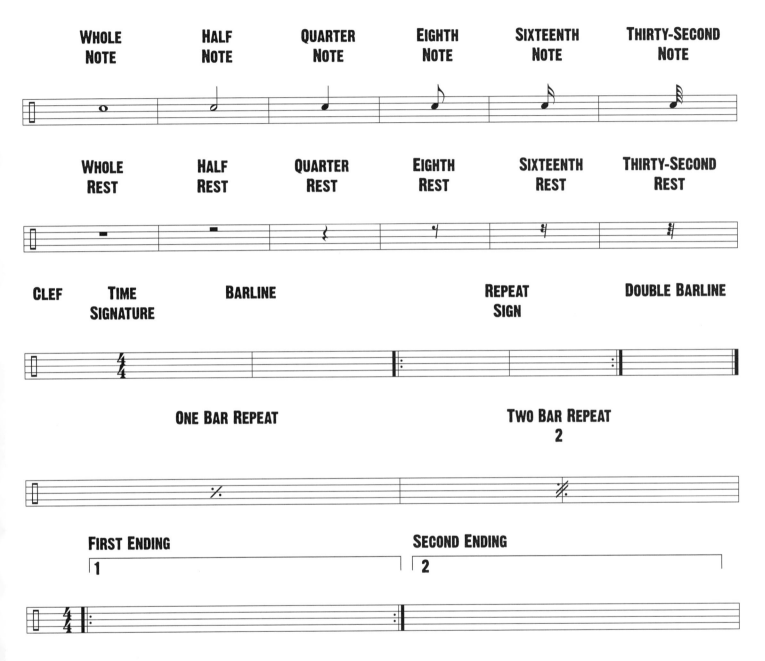

D.C. al FINE / Return to the beginning and play to FINE.

D.S. al FINE / Return to 𝄋 and play to FINE.

D.C. al Coda / Return the the beginning, play to ⊕ and skip to the Coda.

D.S. al Coda / Return to 𝄋, play to ⊕ and skip to the Coda.

PERCUSSIVE ARTS SOCIETY INTERNATIONAL DRUM RUDIMENTS

ALL RUDIMENTS SHOULD BE PRACTICED: OPEN (SLOW) TO CLOSE (FAST) TO OPEN (SLOW) AND/OR AT AN EVEN MODERATE MARCH TEMPO.

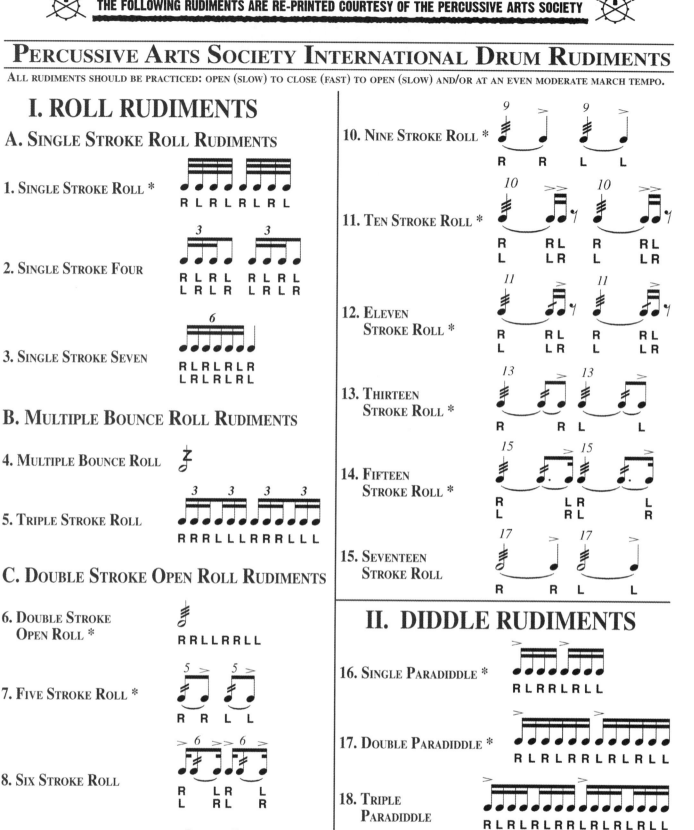

I. ROLL RUDIMENTS

A. SINGLE STROKE ROLL RUDIMENTS

1. SINGLE STROKE ROLL *

2. SINGLE STROKE FOUR

3. SINGLE STROKE SEVEN

B. MULTIPLE BOUNCE ROLL RUDIMENTS

4. MULTIPLE BOUNCE ROLL

5. TRIPLE STROKE ROLL

C. DOUBLE STROKE OPEN ROLL RUDIMENTS

6. DOUBLE STROKE OPEN ROLL *

7. FIVE STROKE ROLL *

8. SIX STROKE ROLL

9. SEVEN STROKE ROLL *

10. NINE STROKE ROLL *

11. TEN STROKE ROLL *

12. ELEVEN STROKE ROLL *

13. THIRTEEN STROKE ROLL *

14. FIFTEEN STROKE ROLL *

15. SEVENTEEN STROKE ROLL

II. DIDDLE RUDIMENTS

16. SINGLE PARADIDDLE *

17. DOUBLE PARADIDDLE *

18. TRIPLE PARADIDDLE

19. SINGLE PARADIDDLE-DIDDLE

* These rudiments are also included in the original Standard 26 American Drum Rudiments.

PERCUSSIVE ARTS SOCIETY INTERNATIONAL DRUM RUDIMENTS

ALL RUDIMENTS SHOULD BE PRACTICED: OPEN (SLOW) TO CLOSE (FAST) TO OPEN (SLOW) AND/OR AT AN EVEN MODERATE MARCH TEMPO.

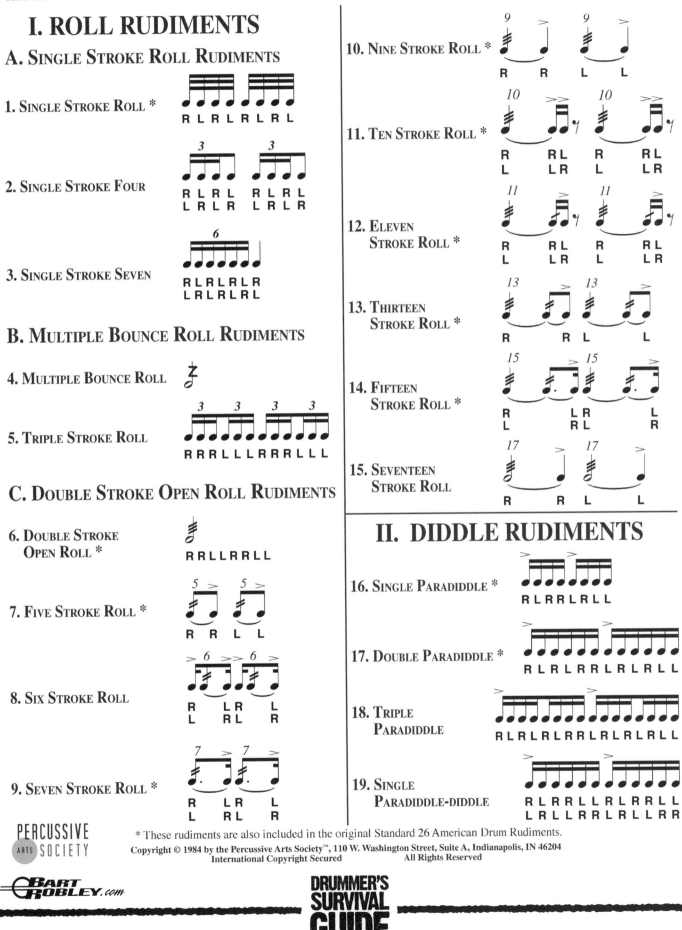

I. ROLL RUDIMENTS

A. SINGLE STROKE ROLL RUDIMENTS

1. SINGLE STROKE ROLL *
2. SINGLE STROKE FOUR
3. SINGLE STROKE SEVEN

B. MULTIPLE BOUNCE ROLL RUDIMENTS

4. MULTIPLE BOUNCE ROLL
5. TRIPLE STROKE ROLL

C. DOUBLE STROKE OPEN ROLL RUDIMENTS

6. DOUBLE STROKE OPEN ROLL *
7. FIVE STROKE ROLL *
8. SIX STROKE ROLL
9. SEVEN STROKE ROLL *

10. NINE STROKE ROLL *
11. TEN STROKE ROLL *
12. ELEVEN STROKE ROLL *
13. THIRTEEN STROKE ROLL *
14. FIFTEEN STROKE ROLL *
15. SEVENTEEN STROKE ROLL

II. DIDDLE RUDIMENTS

16. SINGLE PARADIDDLE *
17. DOUBLE PARADIDDLE *
18. TRIPLE PARADIDDLE
19. SINGLE PARADIDDLE-DIDDLE

* These rudiments are also included in the original Standard 26 American Drum Rudiments.

PERCUSSIVE ARTS SOCIETY

BART ROBLEY.com

DRUMMER'S SURVIVAL GUIDE

One Bar
Eighth Note Rock

Book

_____

_____

_____

_____

_____

Instructions

_____

_____

_____

_____

_____

DVD and Websites

_____

_____

_____

_____

Suggested Listening

_____

_____

_____

_____

Notes

_____

_____

_____

_____

_____

_____

_____

_____

ONE BAR EIGHTH NOTE ROCK

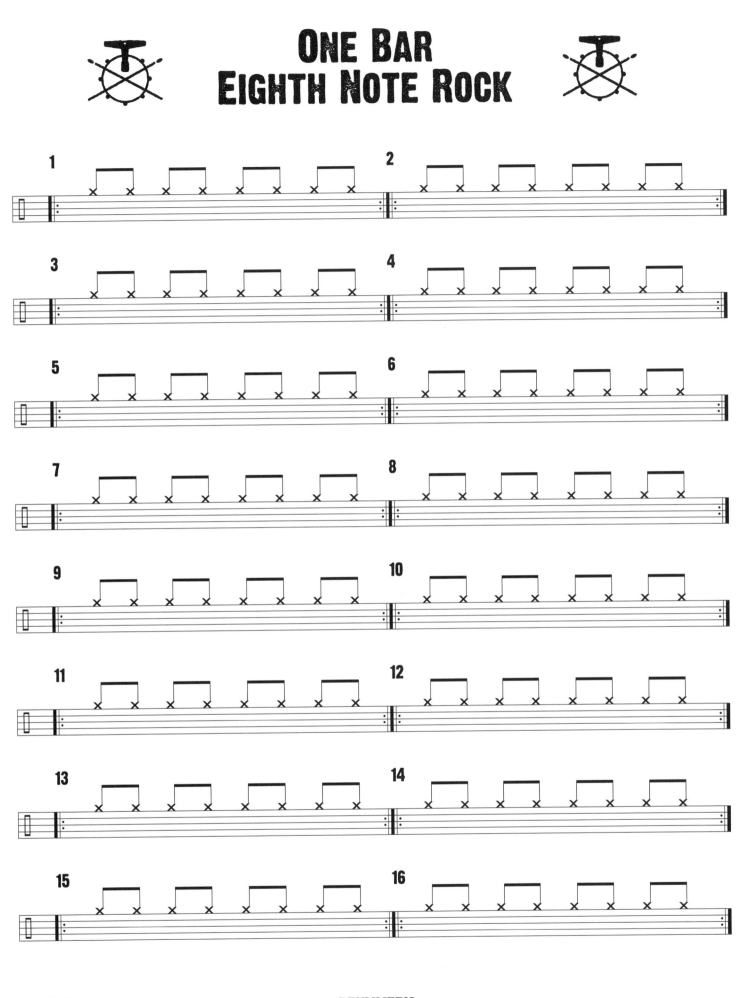

ONE BAR
EIGHTH NOTE ROCK

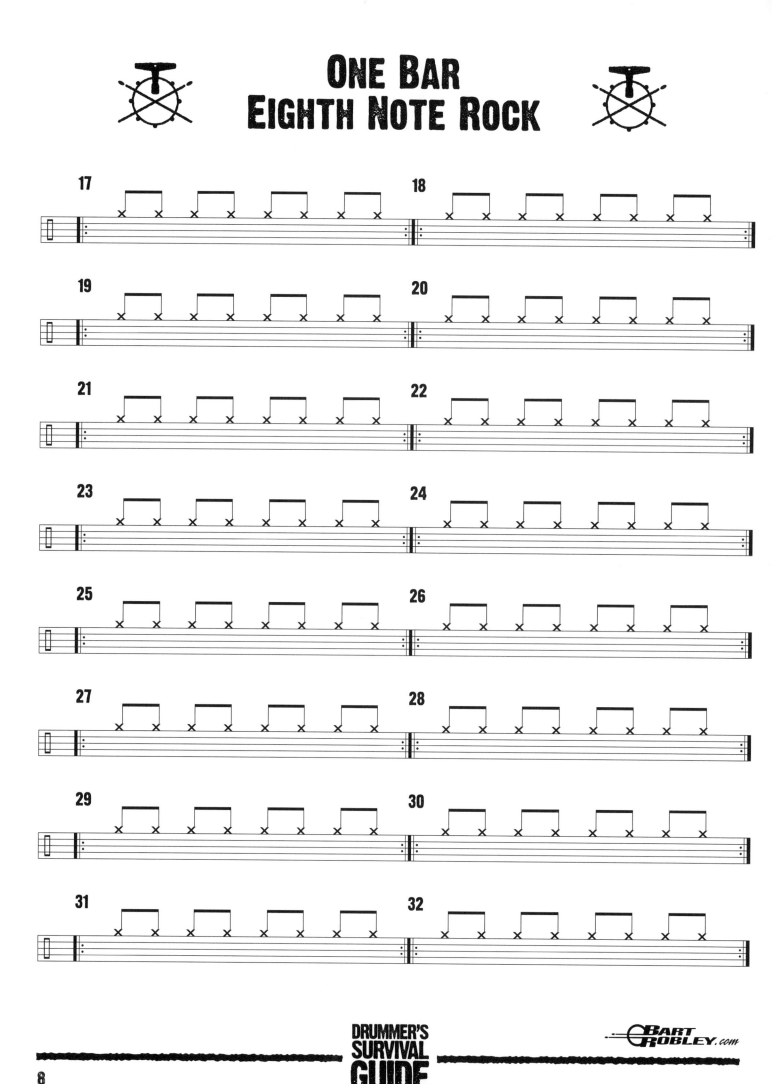

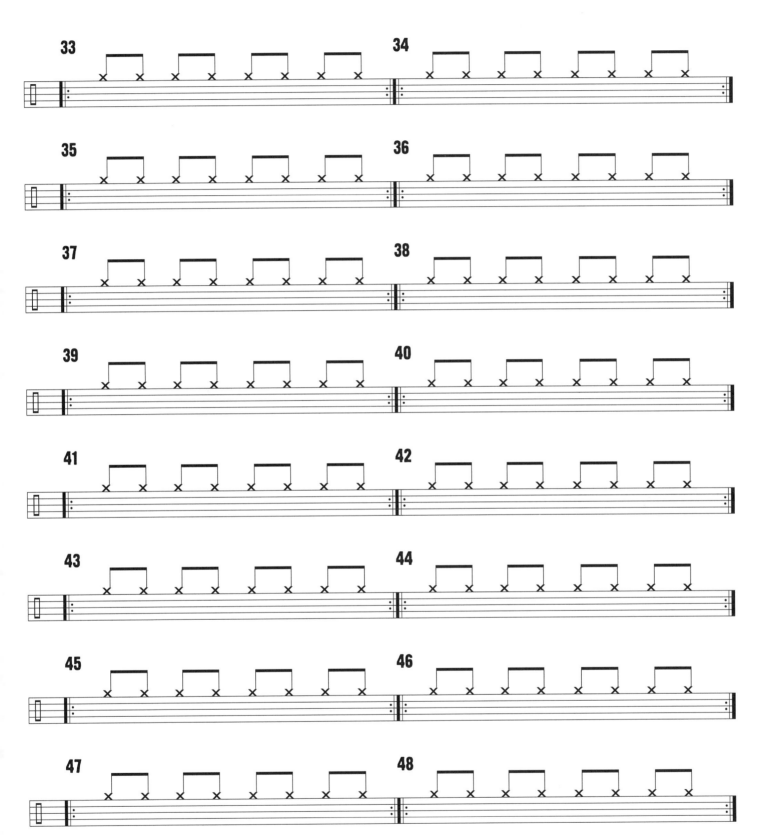

ONE BAR
EIGHTH NOTE ROCK

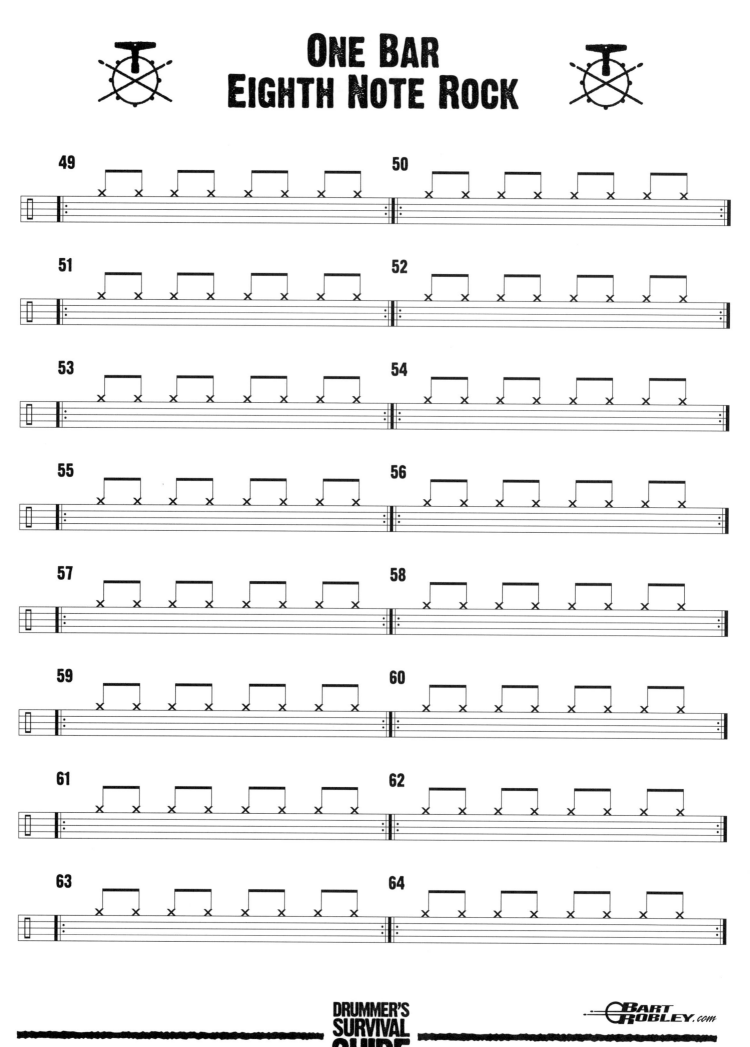

DRUMMER'S
SURVIVAL
GUIDE

BART ROBLEY.com

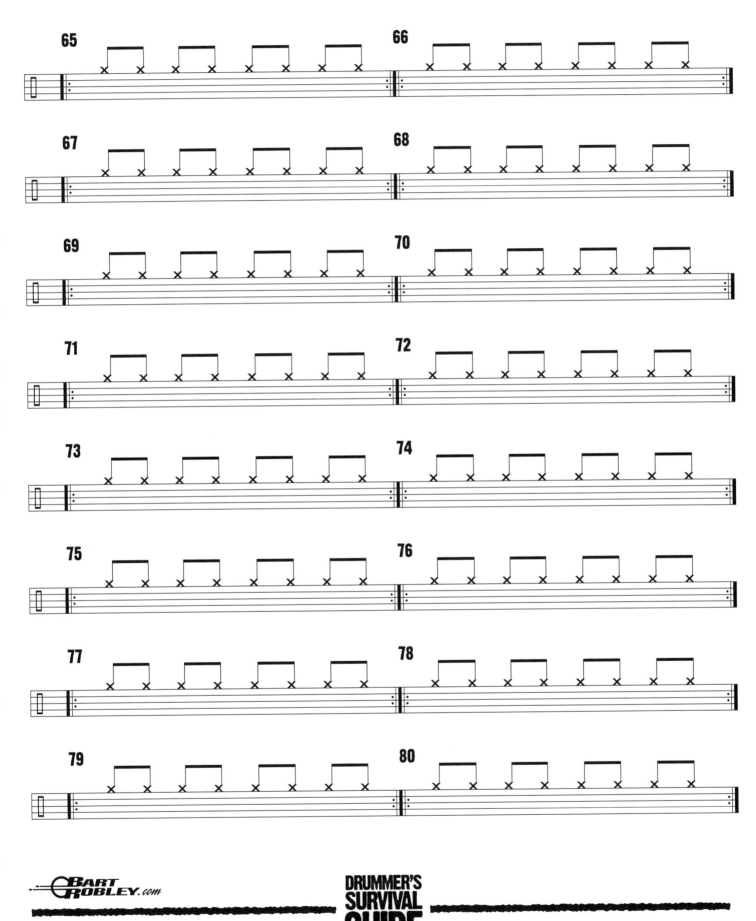

Two Bar
Eighth Note Rock

Book

_____
_____
_____
_____
_____

Instructions

_____
_____
_____
_____
_____

DVD and Websites

_____
_____
_____
_____

Suggested Listening

_____
_____
_____
_____

Notes

_____
_____
_____
_____
_____
_____
_____
_____

DRUMMER'S SURVIVAL GUIDE

BART ROBLEY.com

Two Bar
Eighth Note Rock

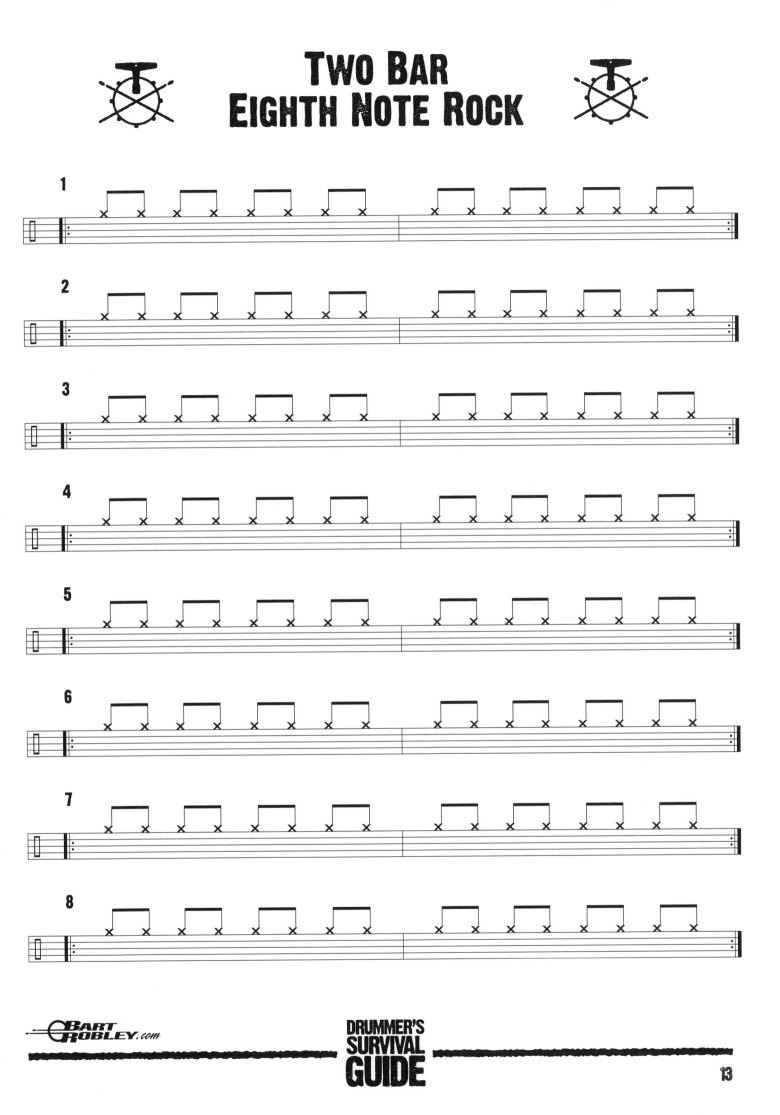

Two Bar Eighth Note Rock

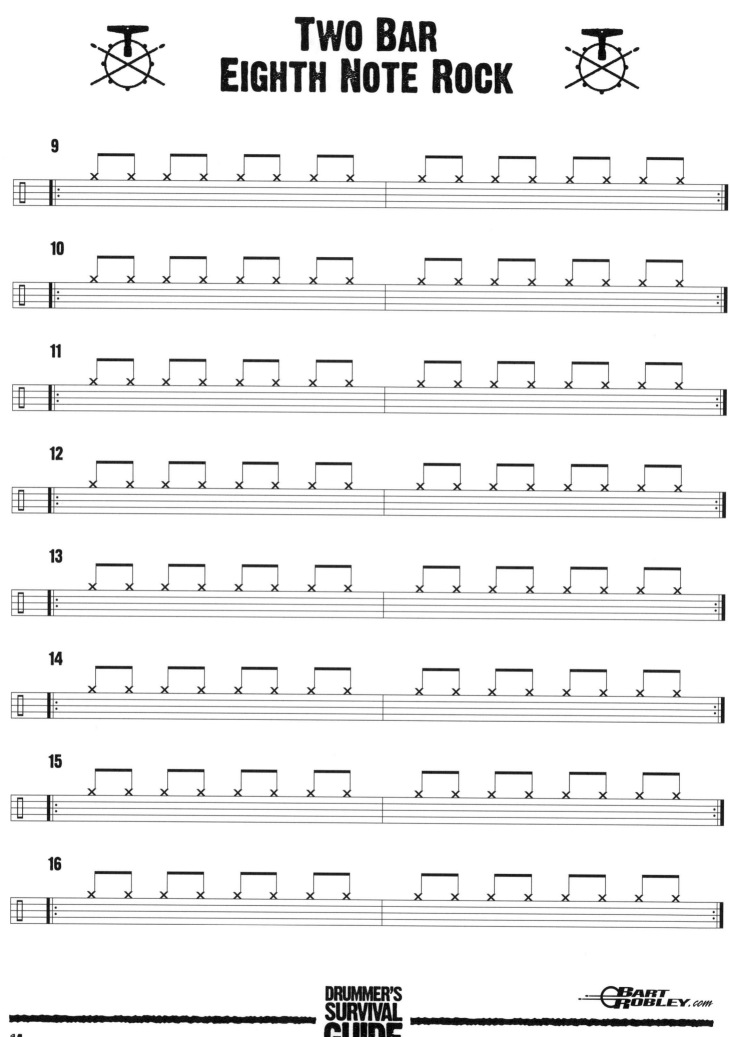

TWO BAR
EIGHTH NOTE ROCK

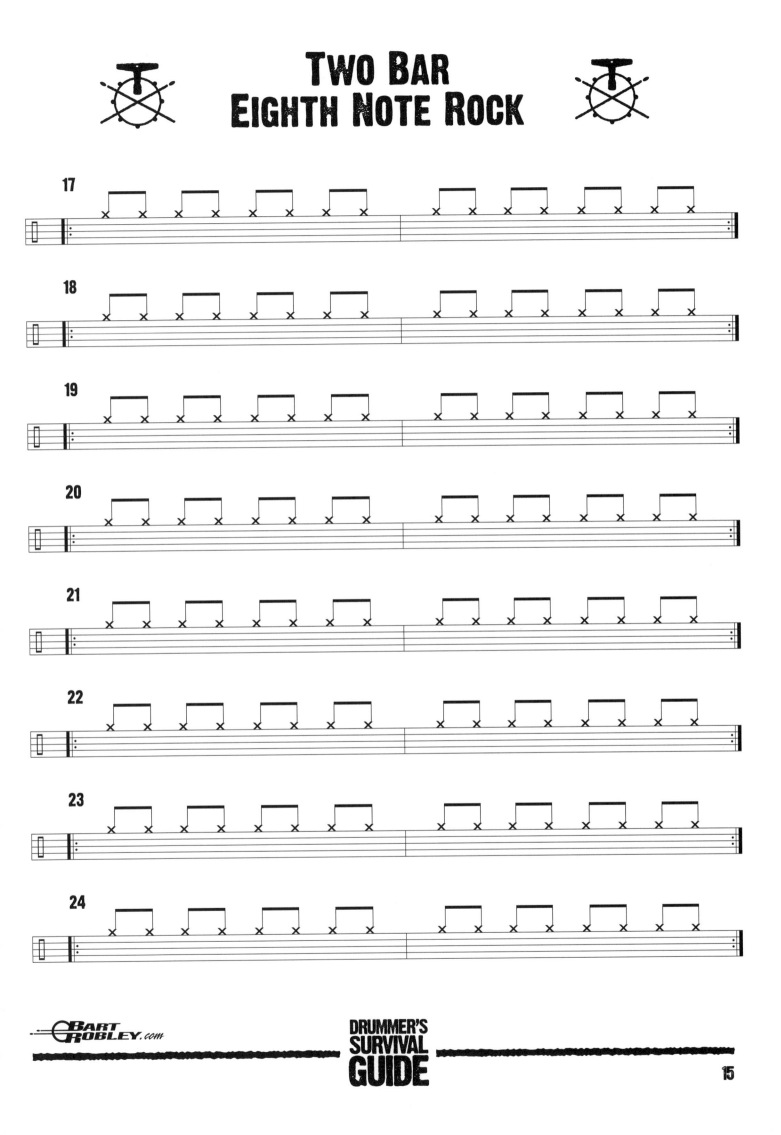

TWO BAR
EIGHTH NOTE ROCK

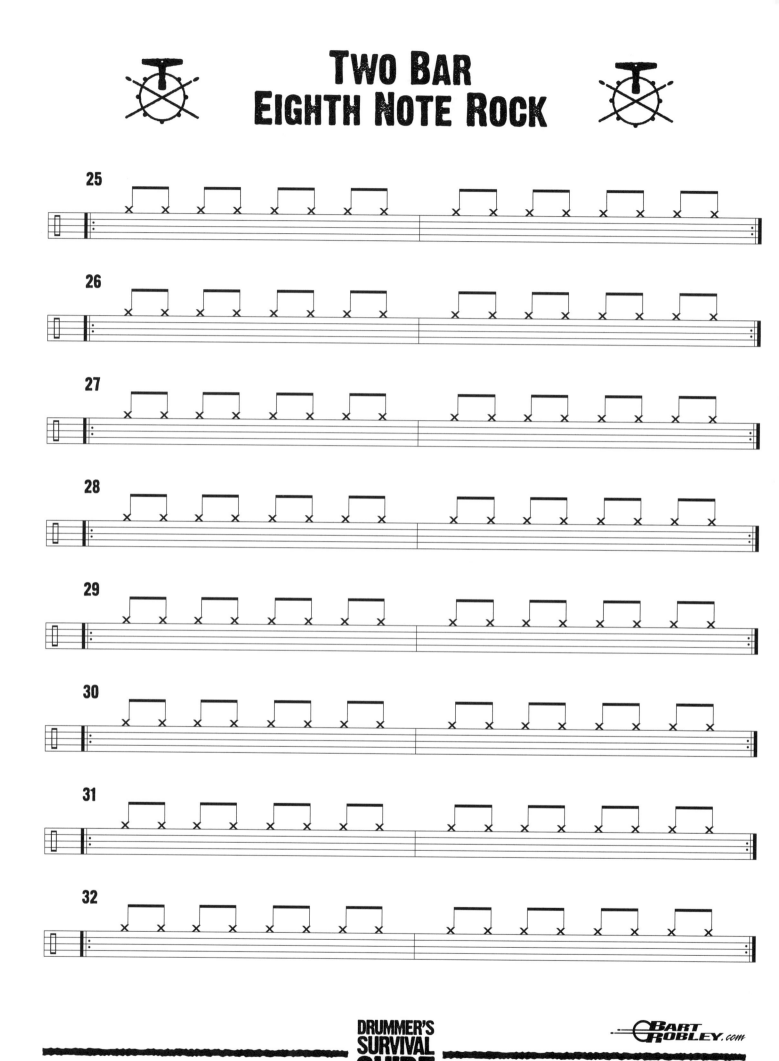

TWO BAR
EIGHTH NOTE ROCK

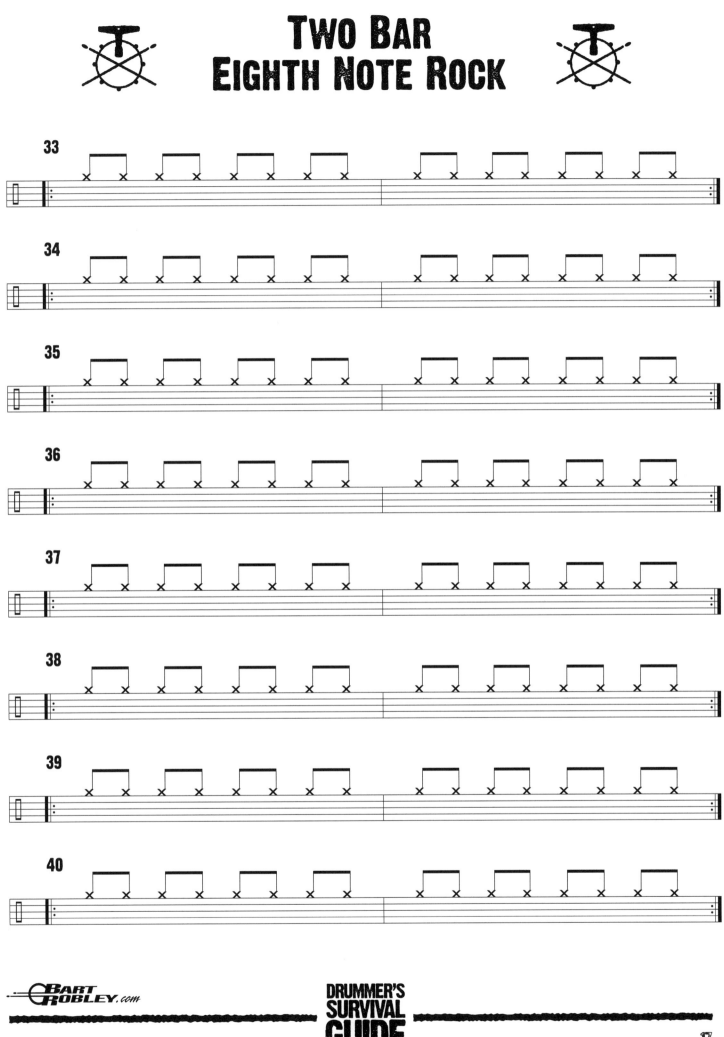

ONE BAR
SIXTEENTH NOTE HI-HAT

BOOK

_____

_____

_____

_____

_____

INSTRUCTIONS

_____

_____

_____

_____

_____

DVD AND WEBSITES

_____

_____

_____

_____

SUGGESTED LISTENING

_____

_____

_____

_____

NOTES

_____

_____

_____

_____

_____

_____

_____

_____

ONE BAR
SIXTEENTH NOTE HI-HAT

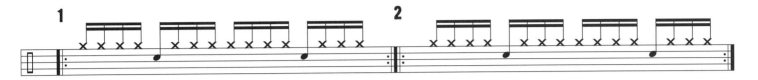

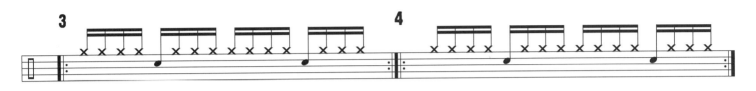

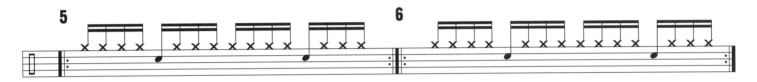

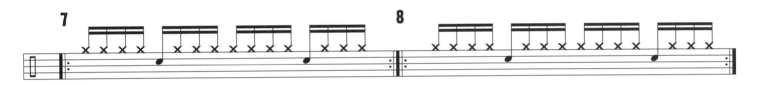

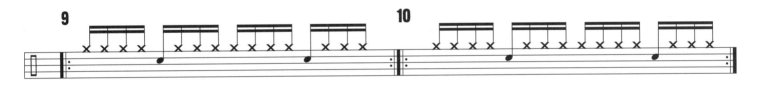

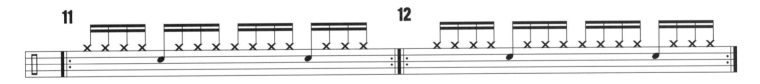

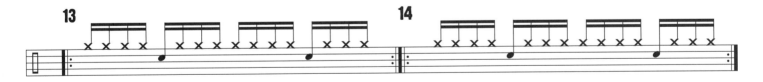

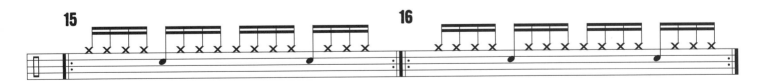

One Bar
Sixteenth Note Hi-Hat

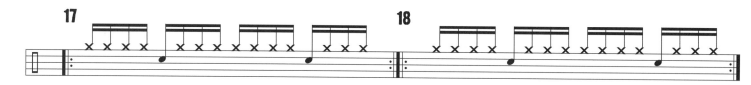

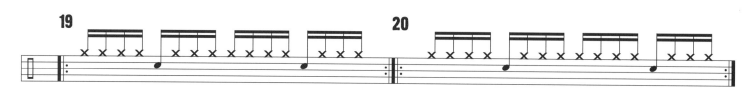

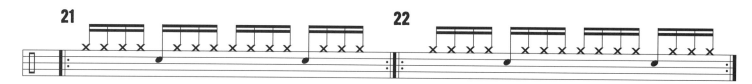

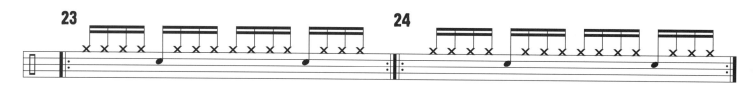

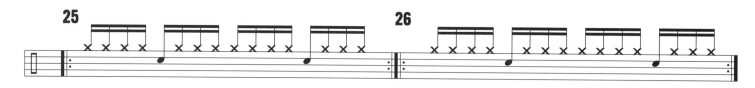

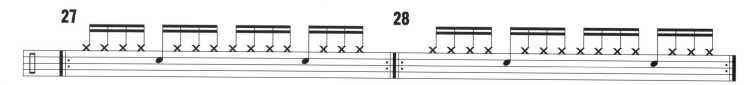

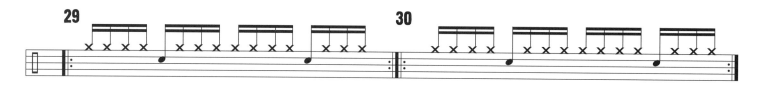

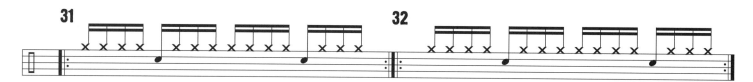

ONE BAR
SIXTEENTH NOTE HI-HAT

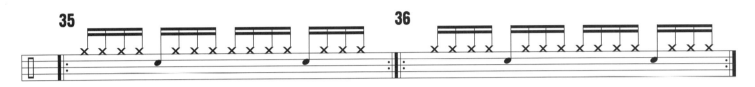

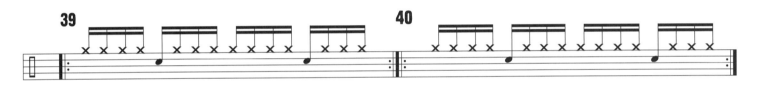

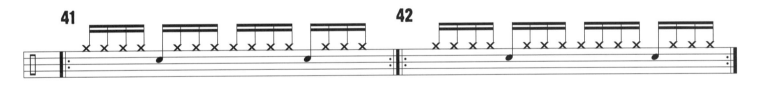

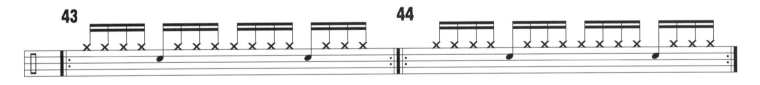

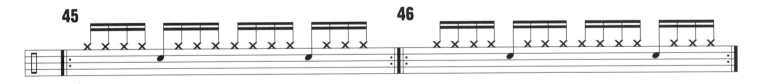

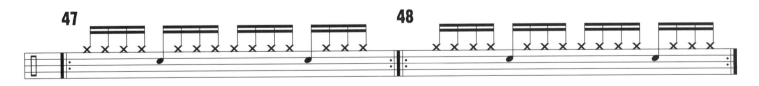

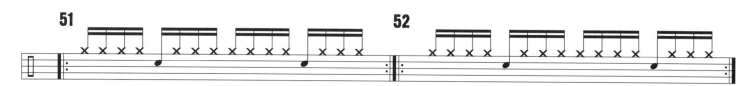

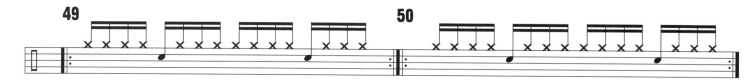

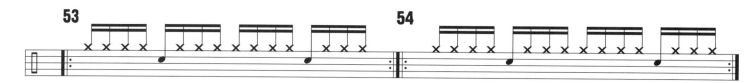

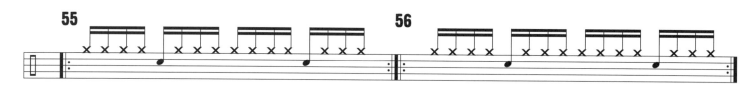

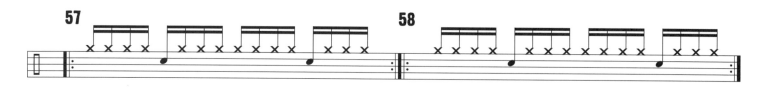

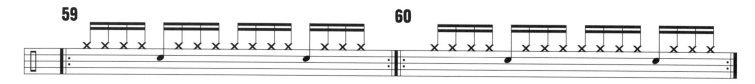

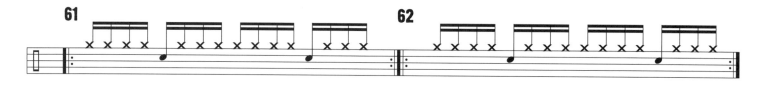

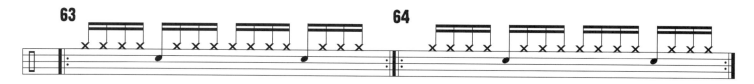

ONE BAR
SIXTEENTH NOTE HI-HAT

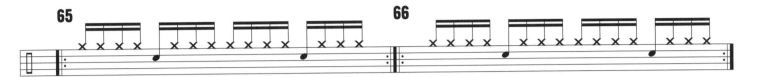

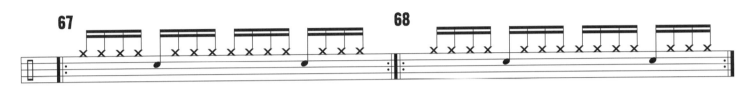

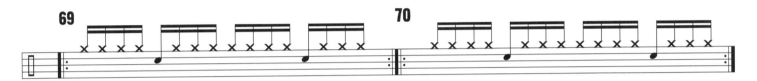

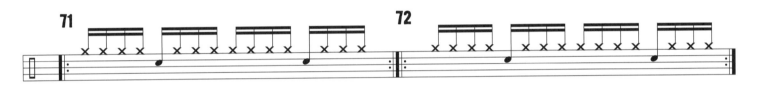

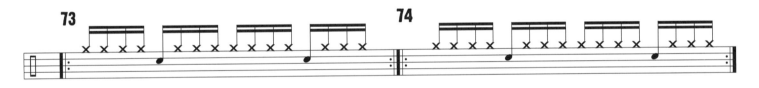

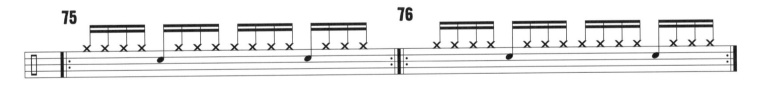

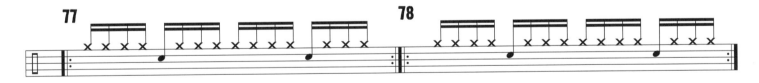

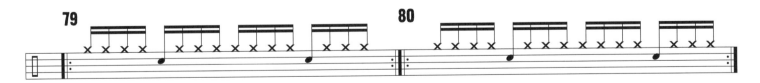

Two Bar
Sixteenth Note Hi-Hat

BOOK

_____

_____

_____

_____

_____

INSTRUCTIONS

_____

_____

_____

_____

_____

_____

DVD AND WEBSITES

_____

_____

_____

_____

SUGGESTED LISTENING

_____

_____

_____

_____

NOTES

_____

_____

_____

_____

_____

_____

_____

_____

Two Bar
Sixteenth Note Hi-Hat

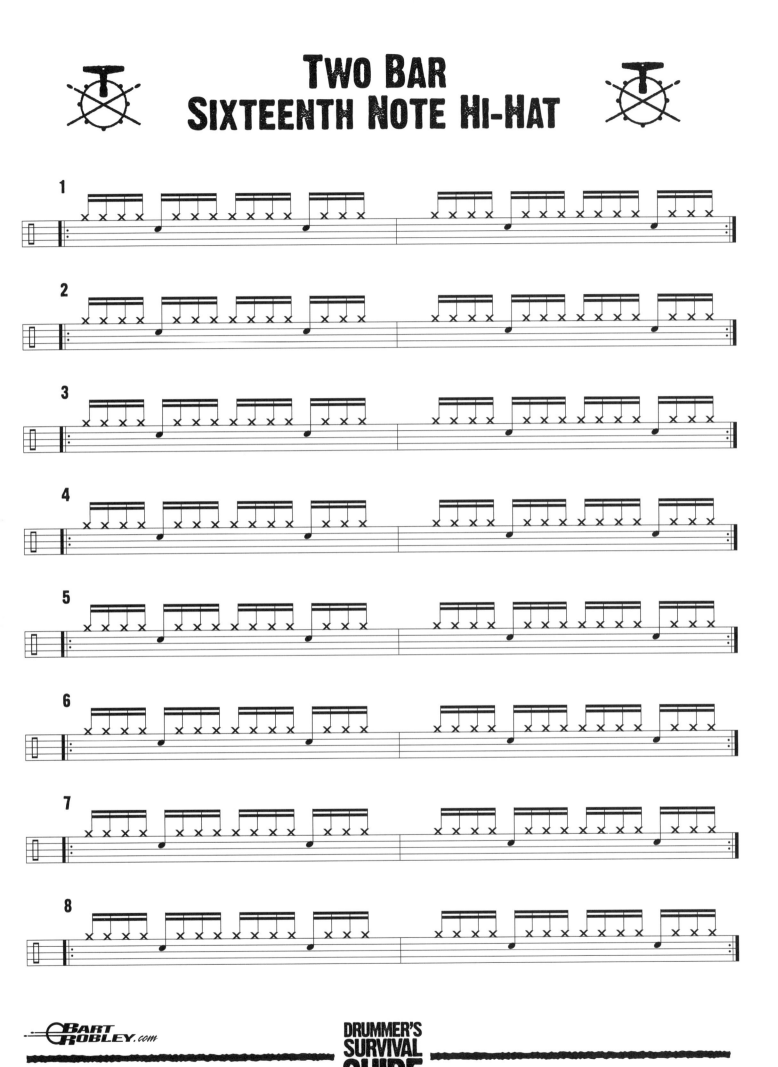

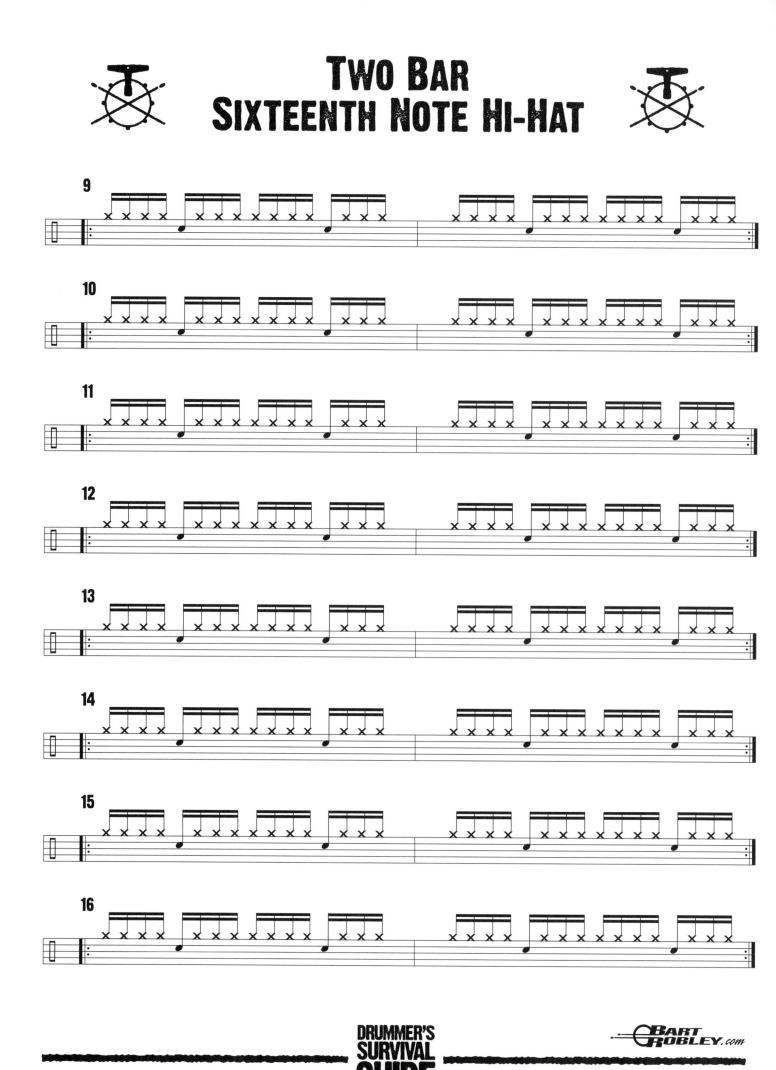

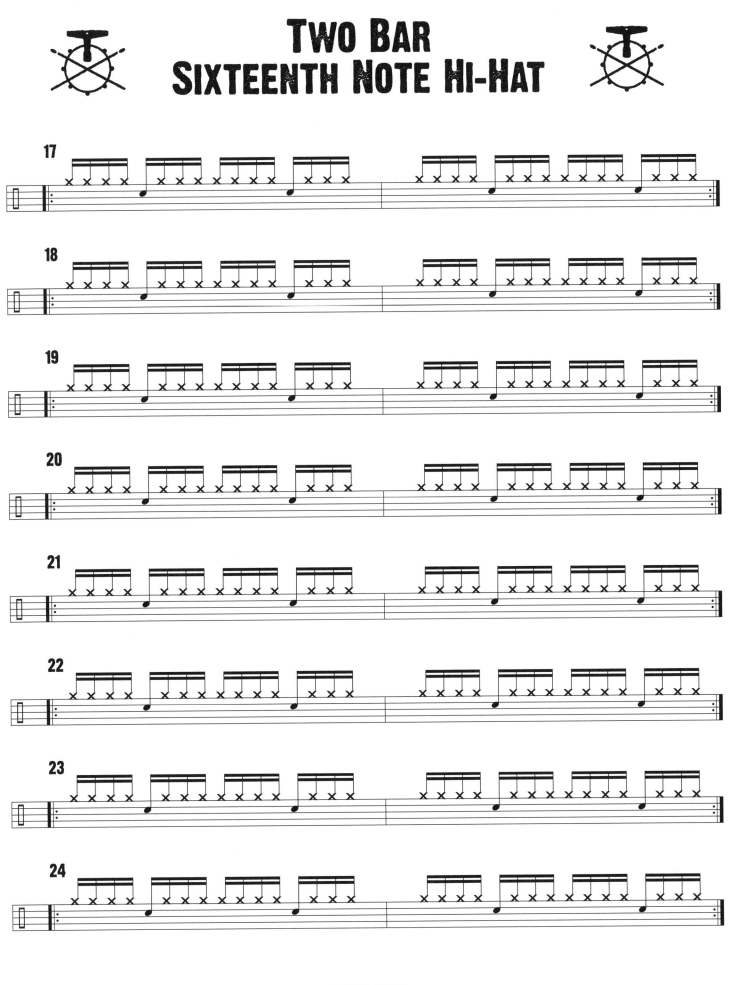

DRUMMER'S
SURVIVAL
GUIDE

25

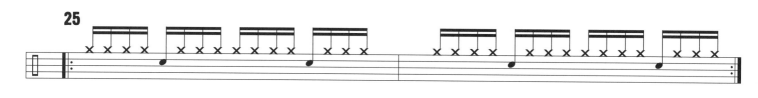

26

27

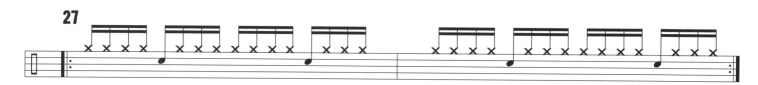

28

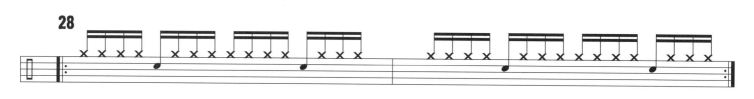

29

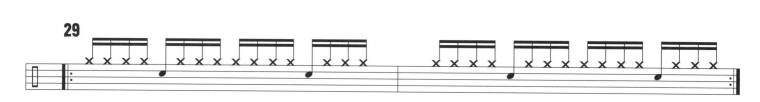

30

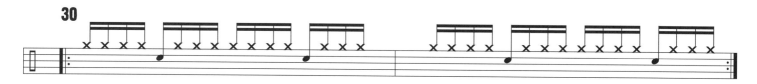

31

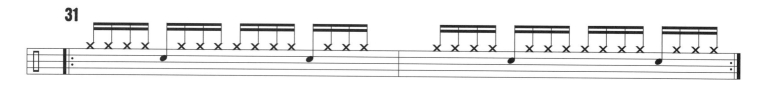

32

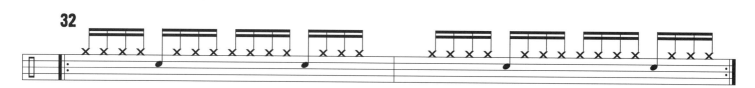

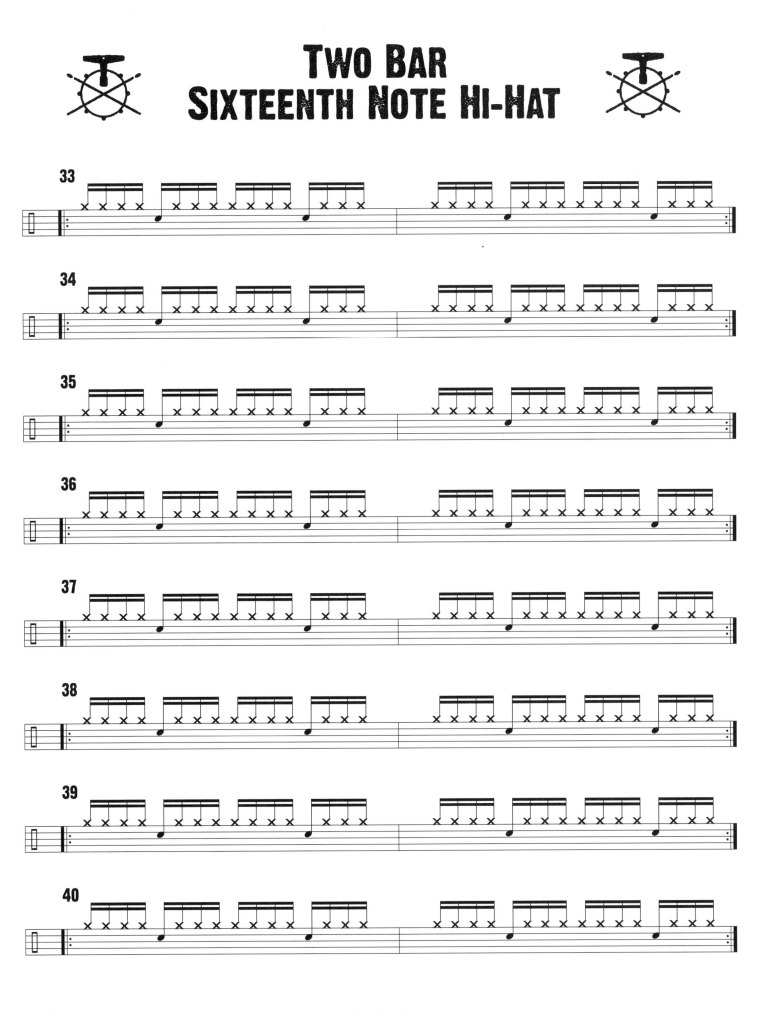

ONE BAR SHUFFLE

Remember, when transcribing a triplet groove, if the second note of the grouping is not played, be sure to include an eighth note rest.

BOOK

_____

_____

_____

_____

_____

INSTRUCTIONS

_____

_____

_____

_____

_____

DVD AND WEBSITES

_____

_____

_____

_____

SUGGESTED LISTENING

_____

_____

_____

_____

NOTES

_____

_____

_____

_____

_____

_____

ONE BAR SHUFFLE

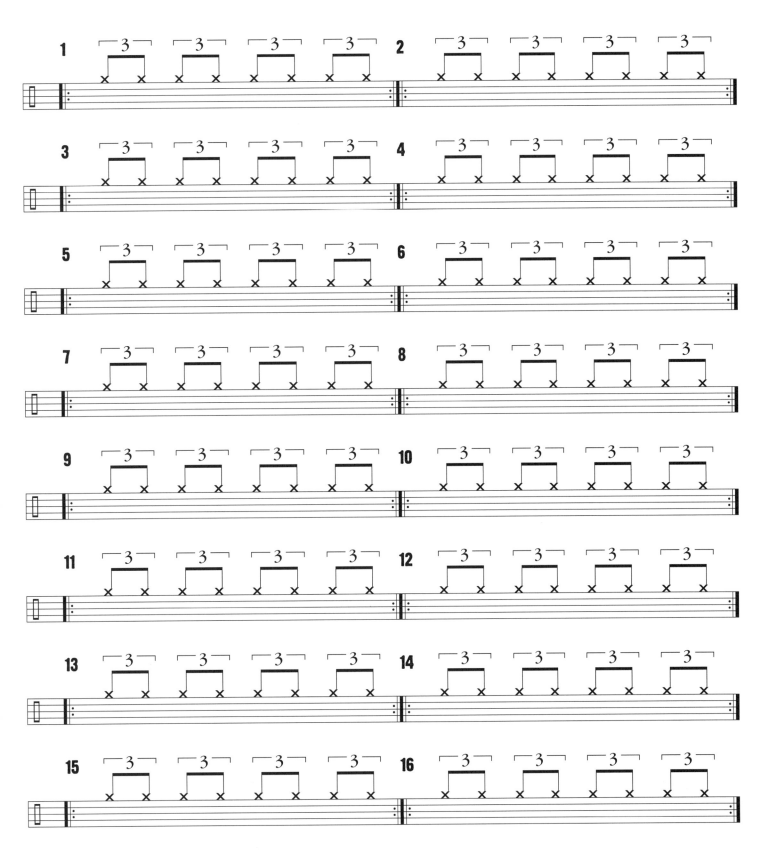

One Bar Shuffle

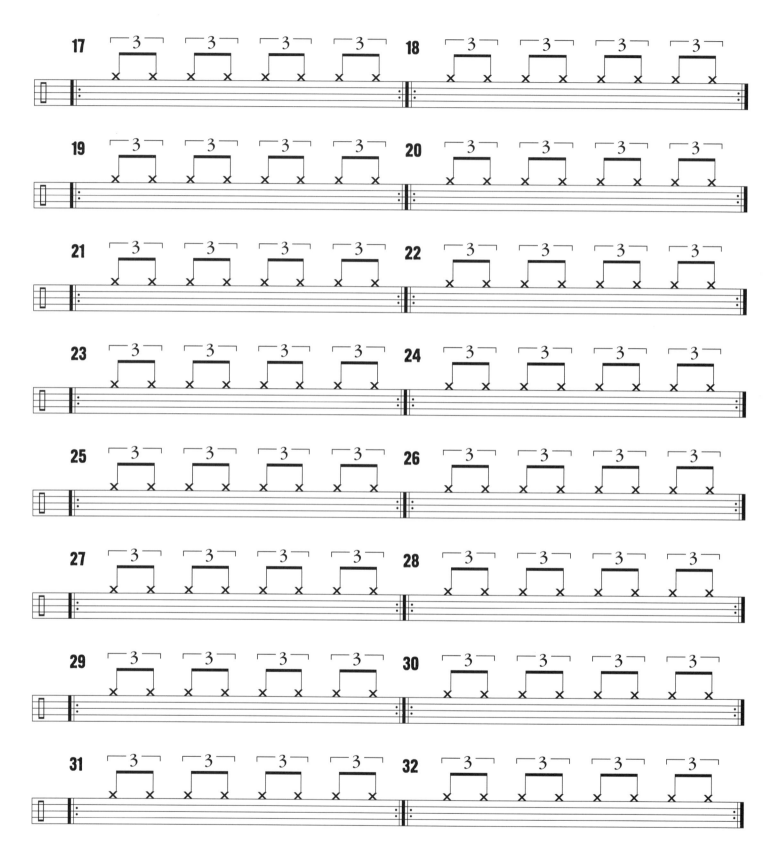

DRUMMER'S SURVIVAL GUIDE

BART ROBLEY.com

ONE BAR SHUFFLE

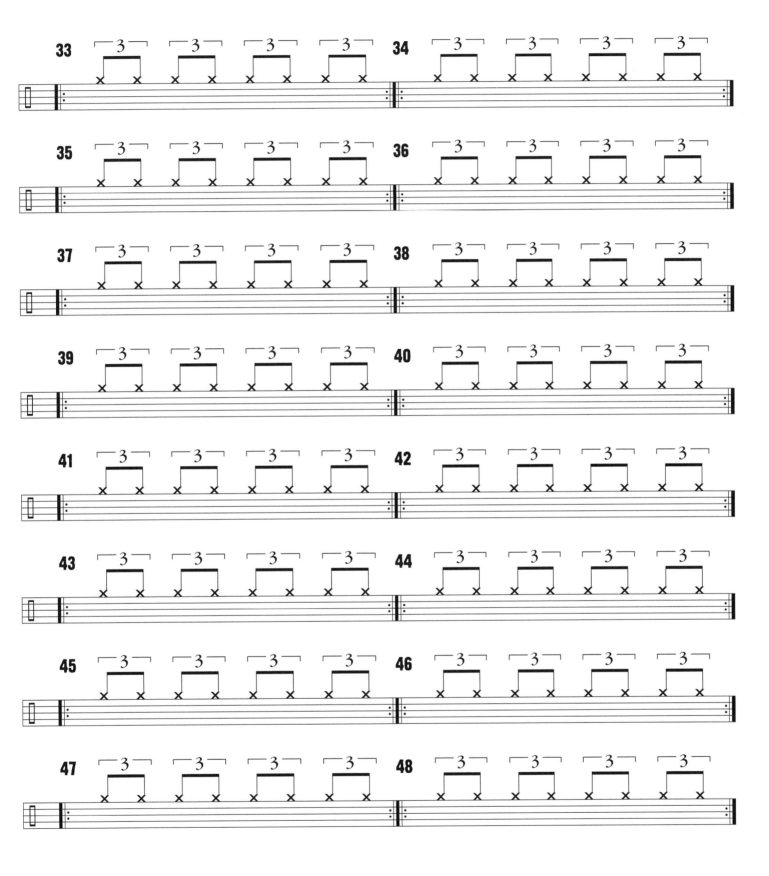

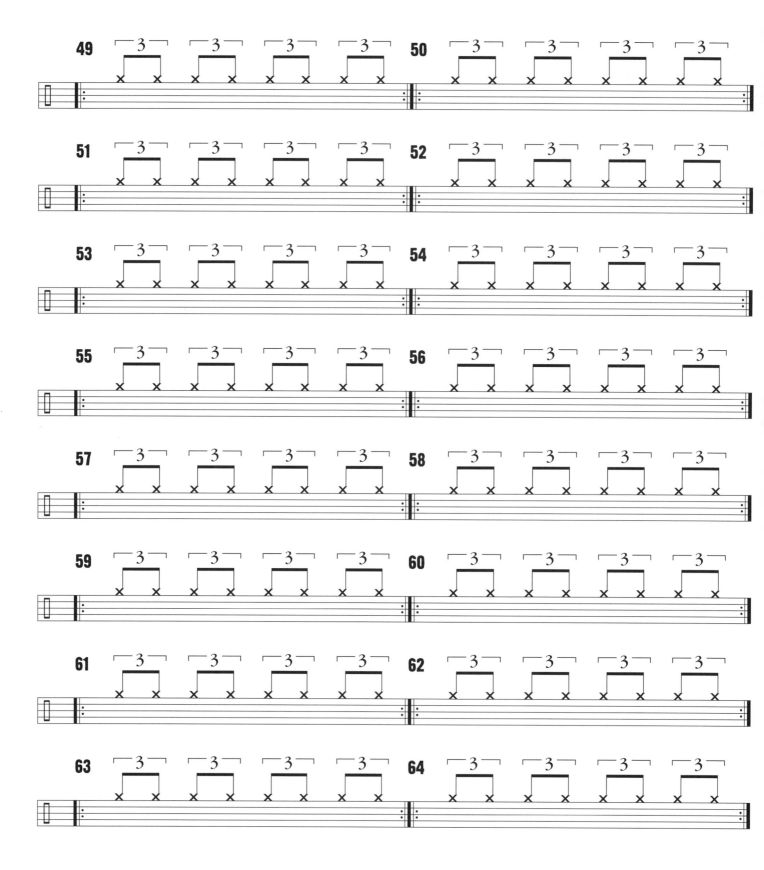

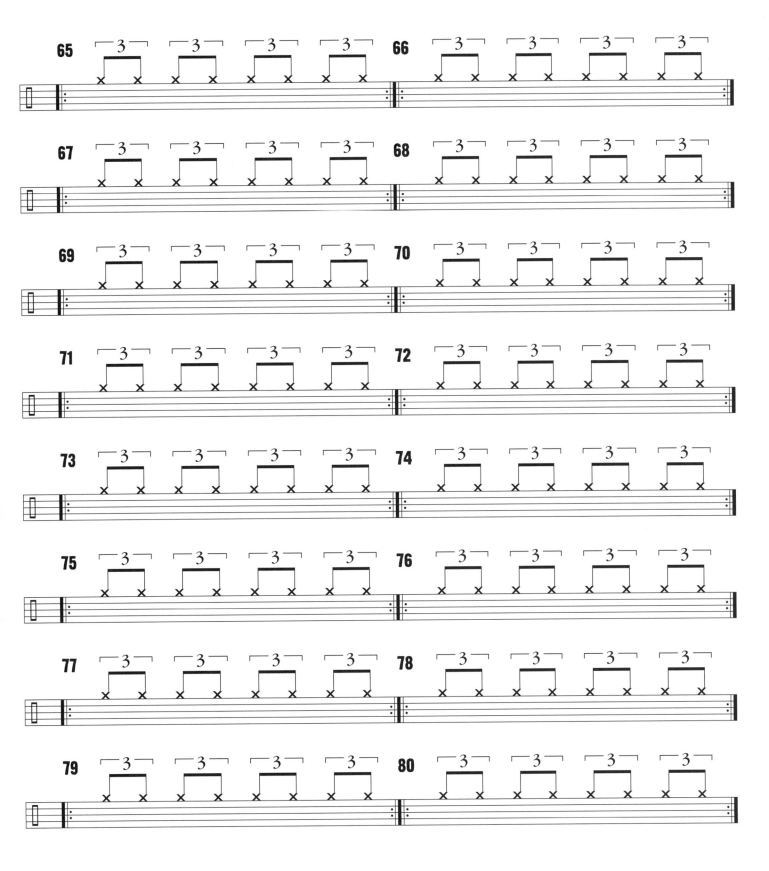

TWO BAR SHUFFLE

Remember, when transcribing a triplet groove, if the second note of the grouping is not played, be sure to include an eighth note rest.

BOOK

_____

_____

_____

_____

_____

INSTRUCTIONS

_____

_____

_____

_____

_____

DVD AND WEBSITES

_____

_____

_____

_____

SUGGESTED LISTENING

_____

_____

_____

_____

NOTES

_____

_____

_____

_____

_____

DRUMMER'S SURVIVAL GUIDE

BART ROBLEY.com

TWO BAR SHUFFLE

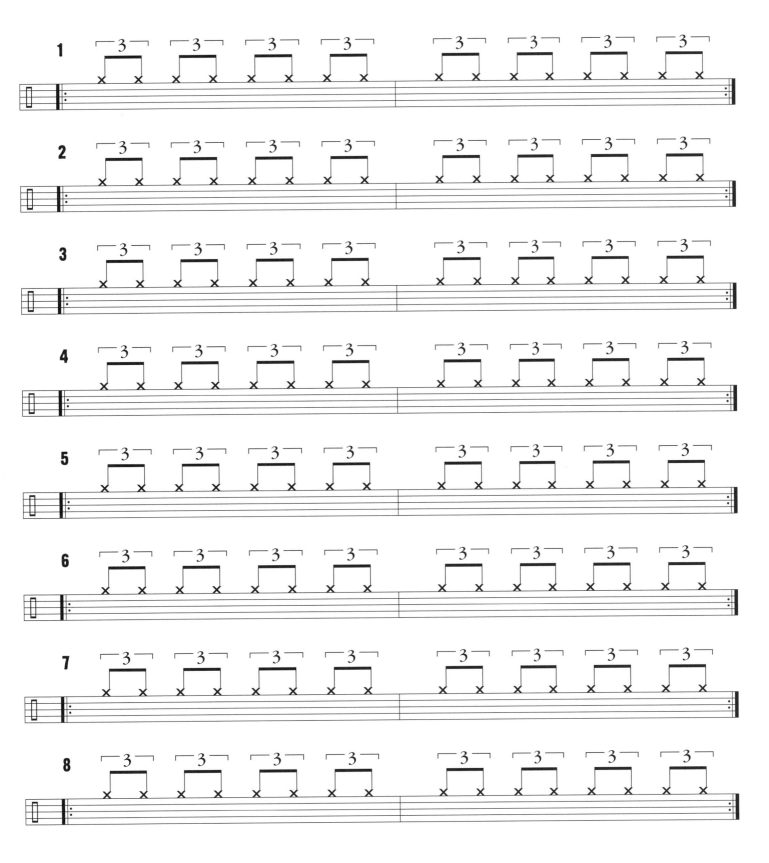

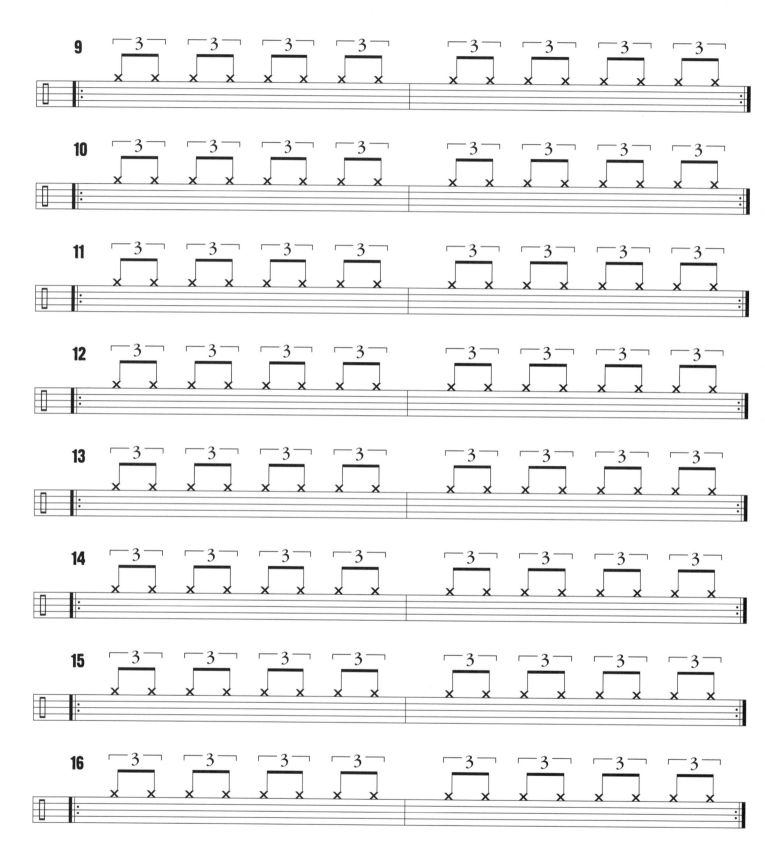

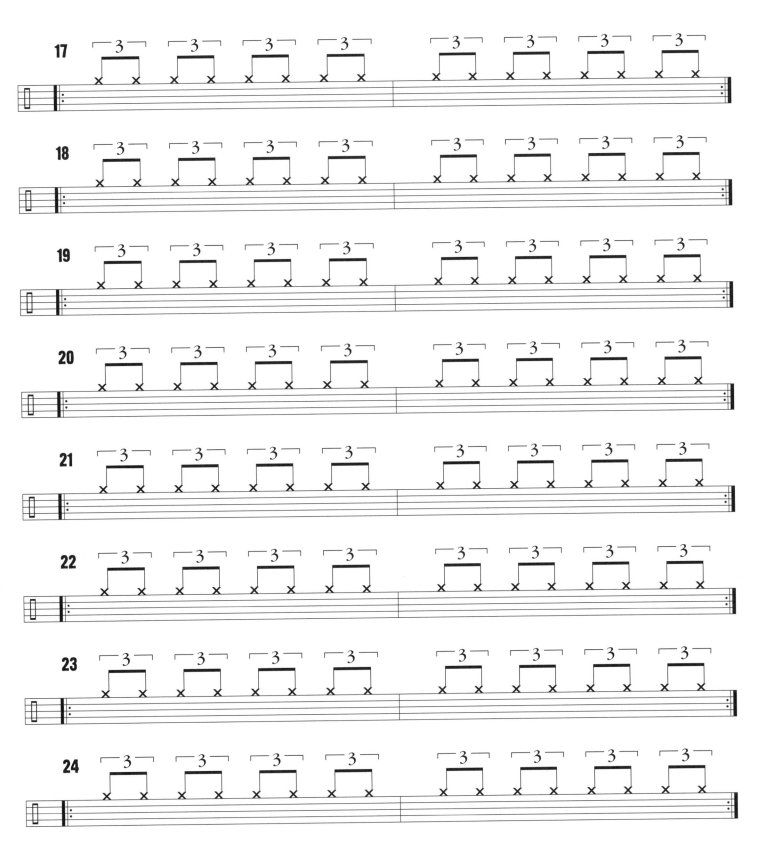

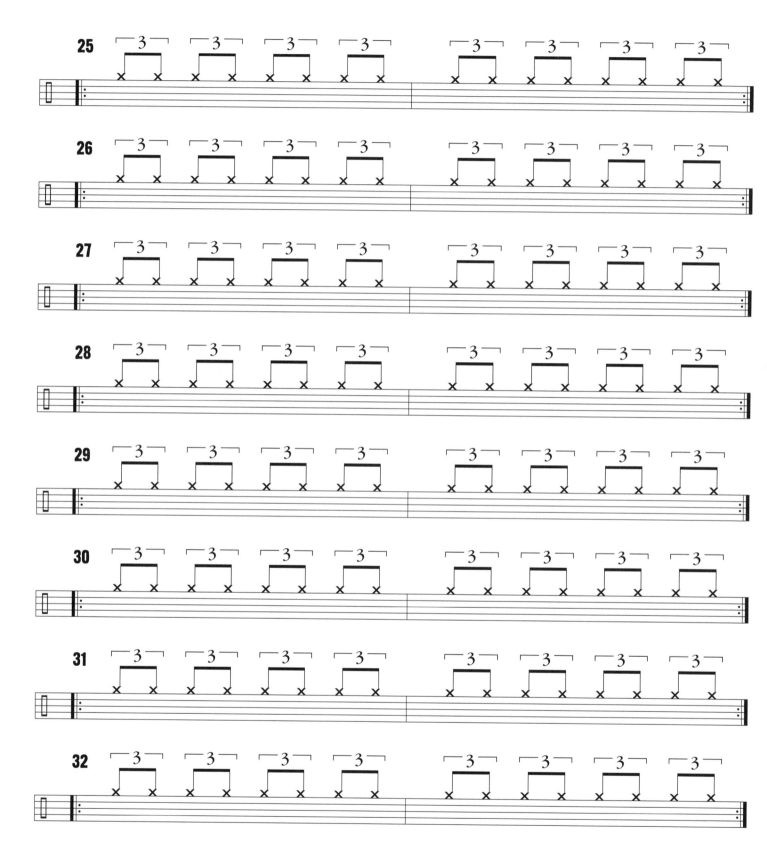

Two Bar Shuffle

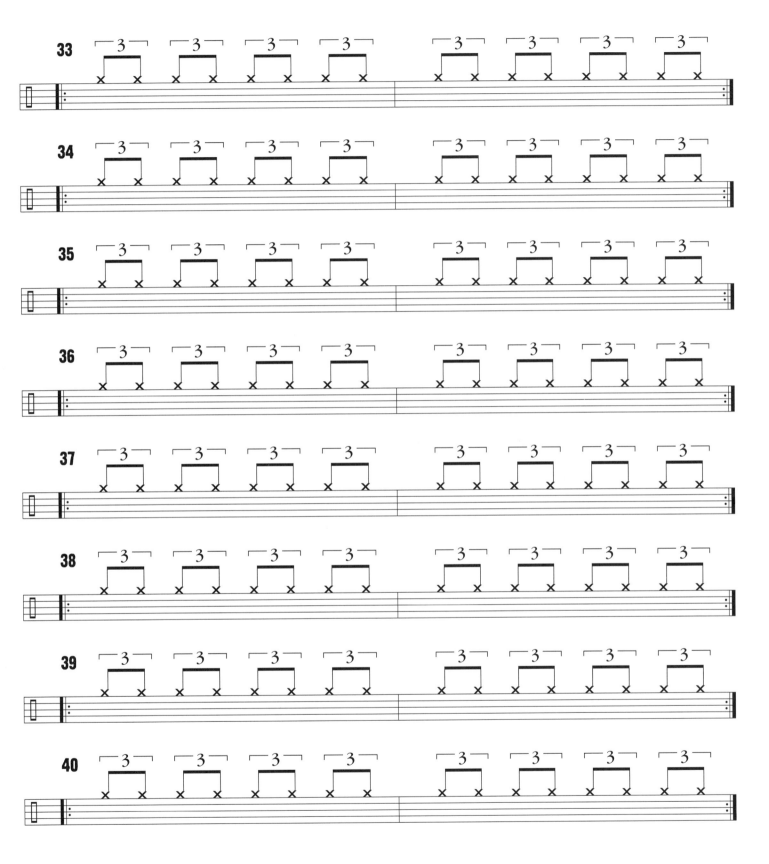

ONE BAR SWING
(JAZZ)

Remember, when transcribing a triplet groove, if the second note of the grouping is not played, be sure to include an eighth note rest.

BOOK

_____

_____

_____

_____

_____

INSTRUCTIONS

_____

_____

_____

_____

_____

DVD AND WEBSITES

_____

_____

_____

_____

SUGGESTED LISTENING

_____

_____

_____

_____

NOTES

_____

_____

_____

_____

_____

_____

ONE BAR SWING
(JAZZ)

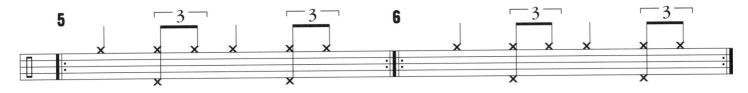

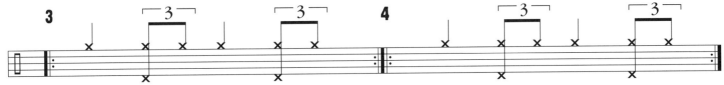

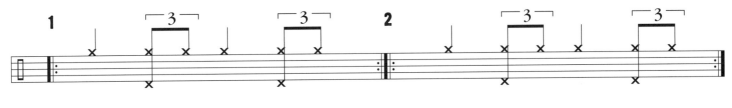

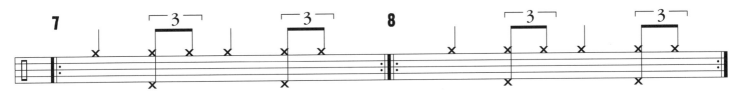

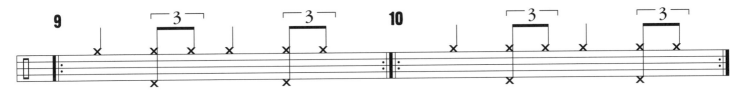

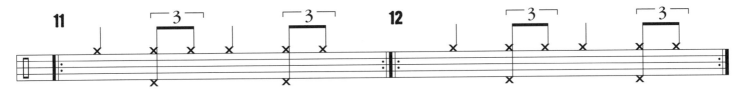

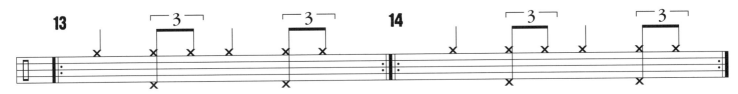

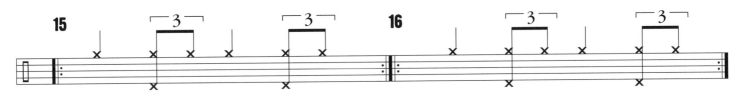

DRUMMER'S SURVIVAL GUIDE

43

ONE BAR SWING
(JAZZ)

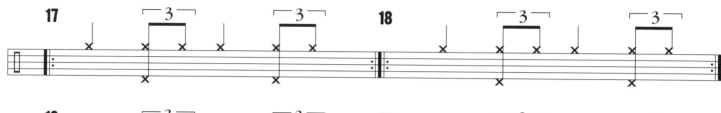

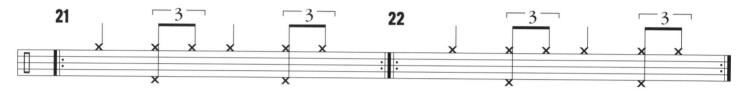

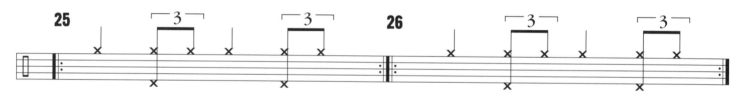

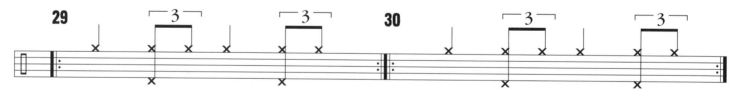

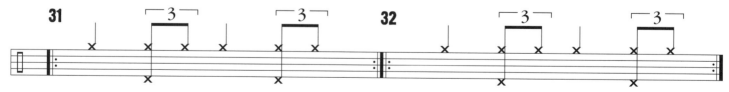

ONE BAR SWING
(JAZZ)

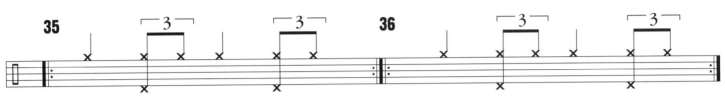

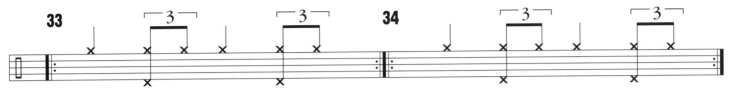

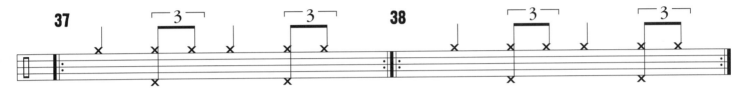

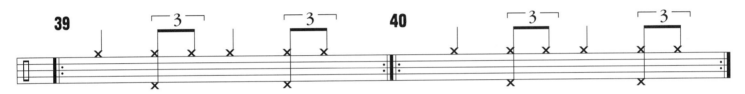

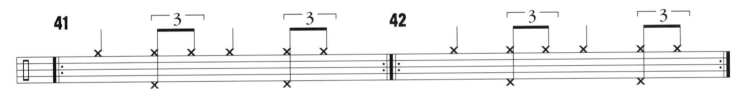

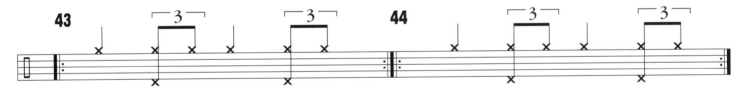

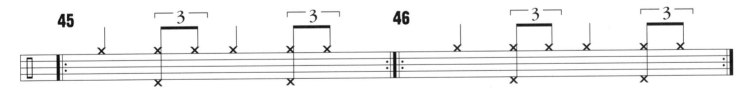

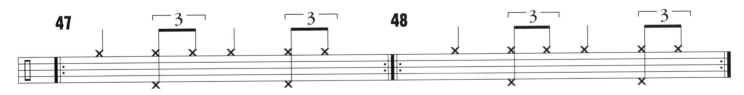

ONE BAR SWING
(JAZZ)

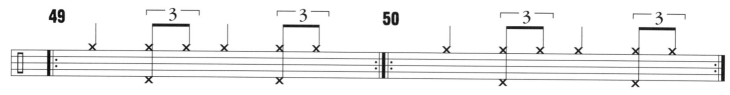

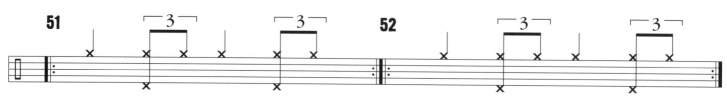

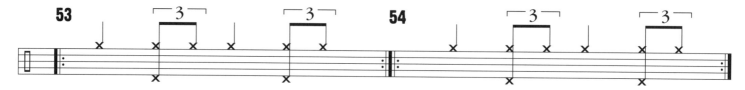

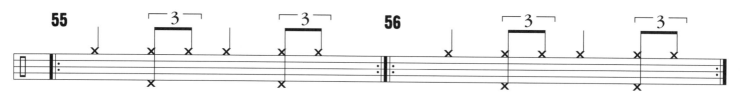

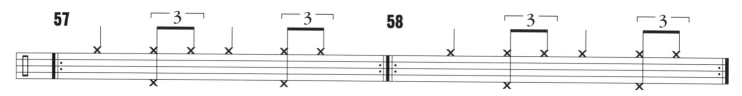

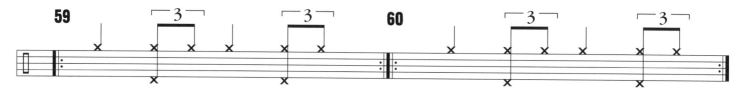

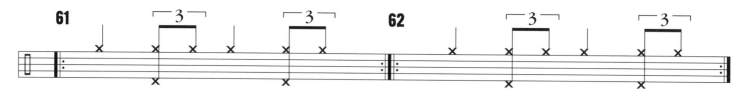

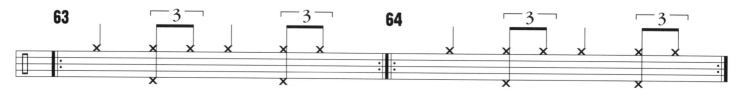

ONE BAR SWING
(JAZZ)

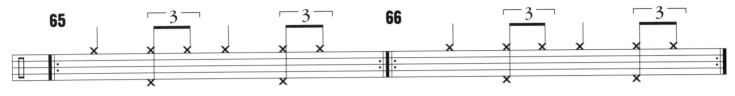

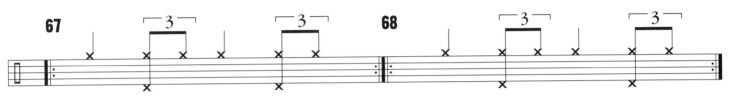

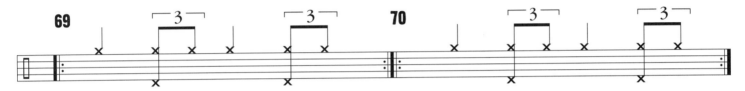

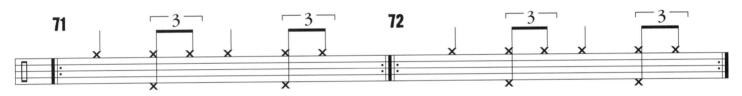

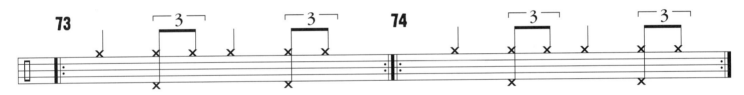

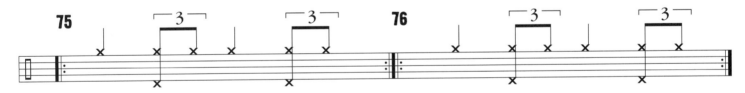

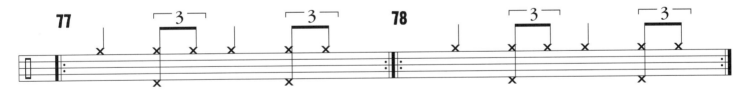

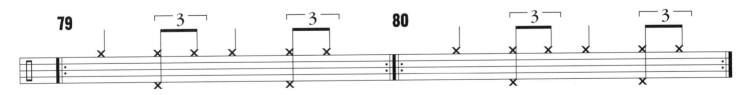

TWO BAR SWING
(JAZZ)

Remember, when transcribing a triplet groove, if the second note of the grouping is not played, be sure to include an eighth note rest.

BOOK

_____

_____

_____

_____

_____

INSTRUCTIONS

_____

_____

_____

_____

_____

DVD AND WEBSITES

_____

_____

_____

_____

SUGGESTED LISTENING

_____

_____

_____

_____

NOTES

_____

_____

_____

_____

_____

_____

DRUMMER'S SURVIVAL GUIDE

BARTROBLEY.com

TWO BAR SWING
(JAZZ)

1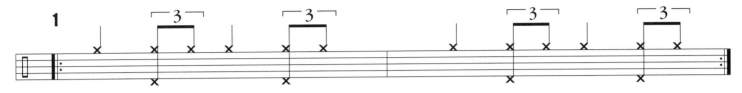

2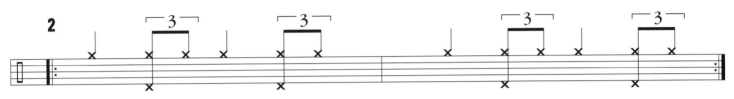

3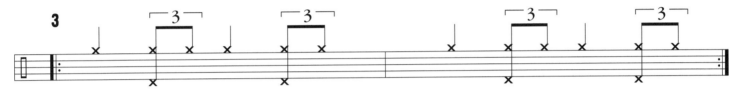

4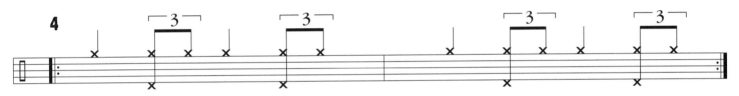

5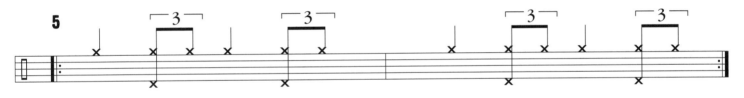

6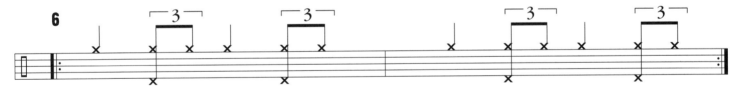

7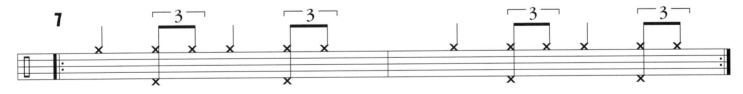

8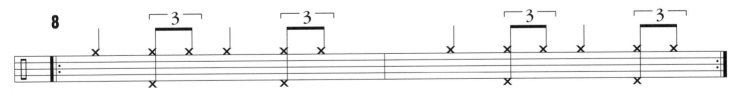

TWO BAR SWING
(JAZZ)

9
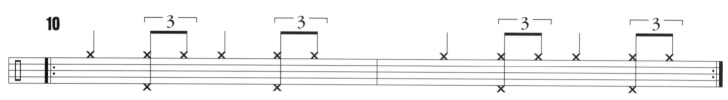

10
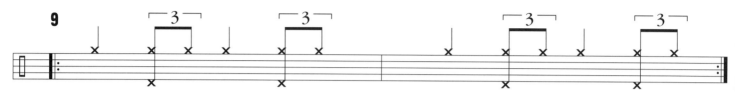

11
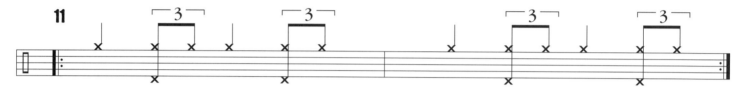

12
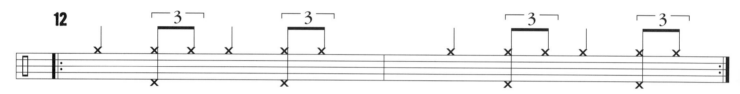

13
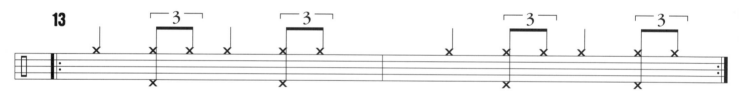

14
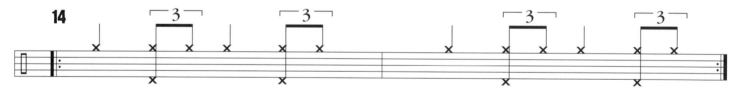

15
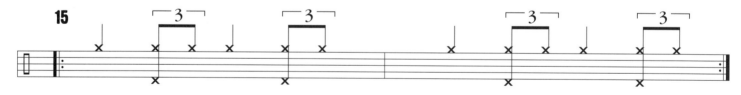

16
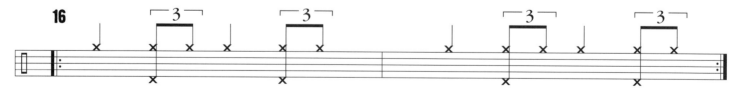

Two Bar Swing
(JAZZ)

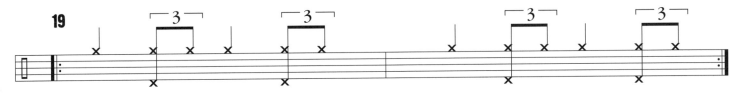

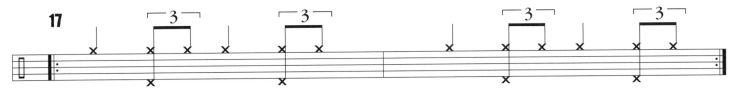

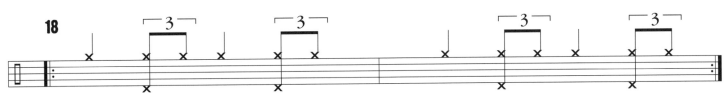

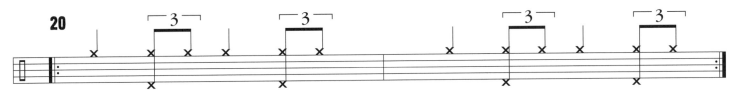

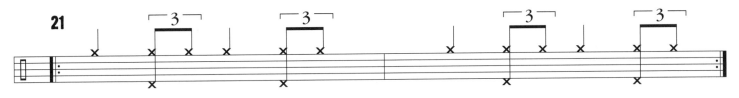

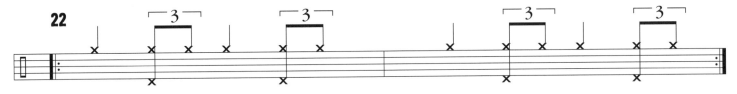

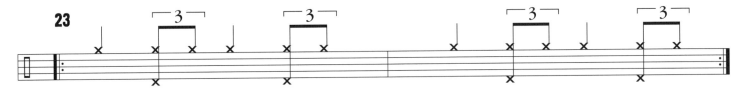

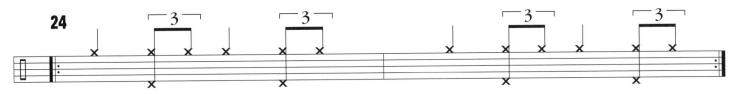

25
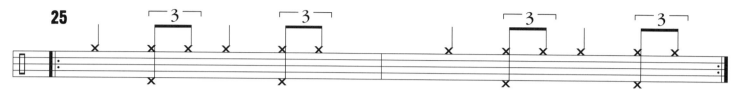

26
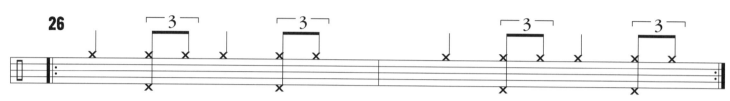

27
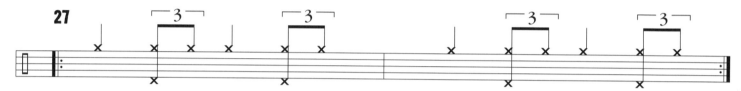

28
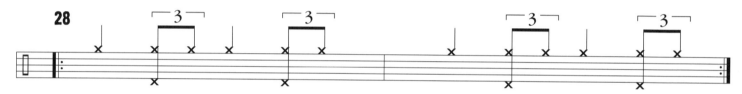

29
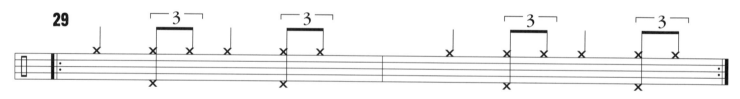

30
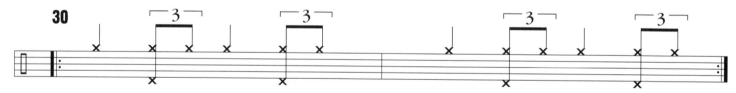

31
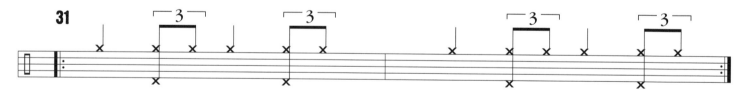

32
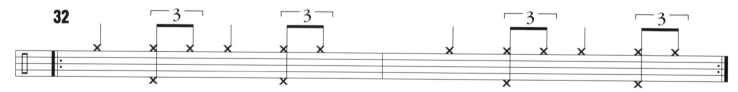

TWO BAR SWING
(JAZZ)

33
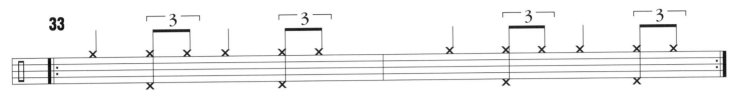

34
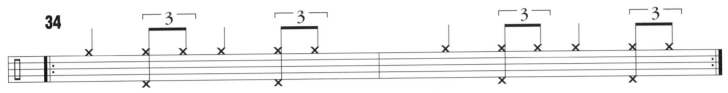

35
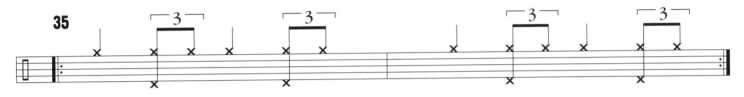

36
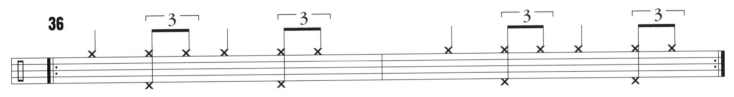

37
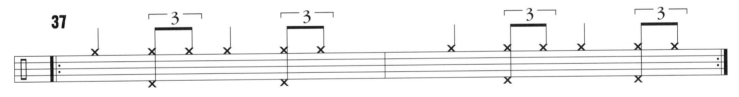

38
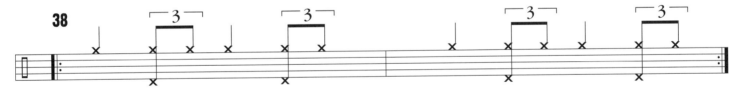

39
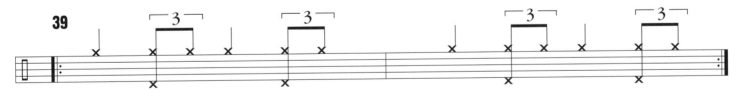

40
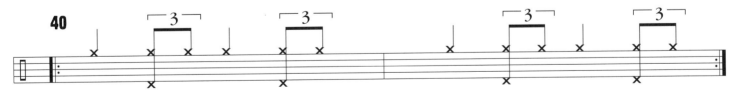

Great Percussion Books from Centerstream...

GRETSCH DRUMS
The Legacy of That Great Gretsch Sound
by Chet Falzerano
This tribute to Gretsch kits features full-color photos and interviews with
sensational players.
00000176 144 pages $34.95

GUIDE TO VINTAGE DRUMS
by John Aldridge
Written by the publisher of Not So Modern Drummer magazine, this in an
essential guide for collectors-to-be that want to shop around, or for cur-
rent collectors to discover drums outside of their area of interest.
00000167 176 pages $24.95

HISTORY OF THE LUDWIG DRUM COMPANY
by Paul William Schmidt
This book uses extensive interviews with the Ludwigs and photos from their
personal collections to recall the origins, development and tools of crafting
drums. You'll also discover why the best drummers use Ludwigs. Over 150
photos and illustrations make this an invaluable reference source for all
drummers.
00000132 172 pages $29.95

THE COMPLETE HISTORY OF
THE LEEDY DRUM COMPANY
by Rob Cook
This is the fascinating story of professional drummer, inventor, and industri-
alist Ulysses Leedy and his apartment-based drum company that became
the world's largest manufacturer of percussion equipment.
00000160 182 pages...$35.00

BILLY GLADSTONE, DRUMMER & INVENTOR
by Chet Falzerano
Admired by colleagues and the public alike, Billy Gladstone was the featured
percussionist at New York's Radio City Music Hall for 18 years after its open-
ing in 1932. He was also a consummate inventor, with more than 20 US
patents to his name, not the least of which was the famous Gladstone snare
drum.
00001027 ....$19.95

P.O. Box 17878 - Anaheim Hills, CA 92817
(714) 779-9390   www.centerstream-usa.com

More Great Percussion Books from Centerstream...